TEENAGE MUTANT TURTLES®

HOW IT ALL BEGAN
AN ADVENTURE TO COLOR

Illustrated by Fernando Fernandez

Adapted from a teleplay by David Wise and Patti Howeth
Based on the Teenage Mutant Ninja Turtles characters
and comic book created by Kevin Eastman and Peter Laird

RANDOM HOUSE
Happy House Group

Published in the United States by Random House, Inc., New York, and simultaneously in Canada by Random House of Canada Limited, Toronto.
ISBN: 0-394-89481-2

Manufactured in the United States of America

Television reporter April O'Neil is on location with her camera crew.

Scientific companies are being robbed of very specialized equipment.

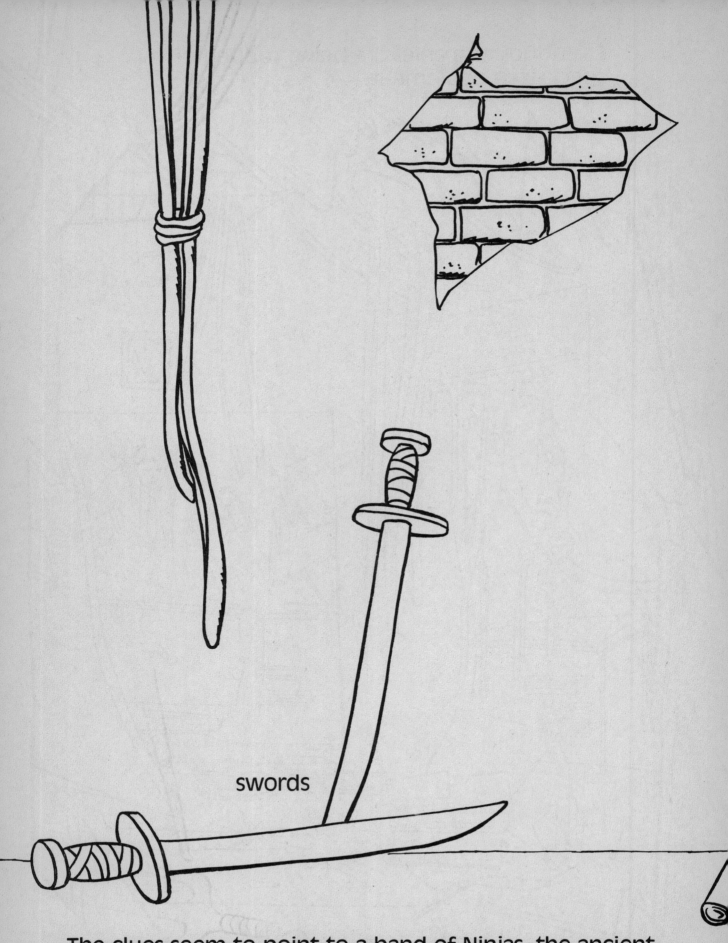

swords

The clues seem to point to a band of Ninjas, the ancient Japanese warrior cult.

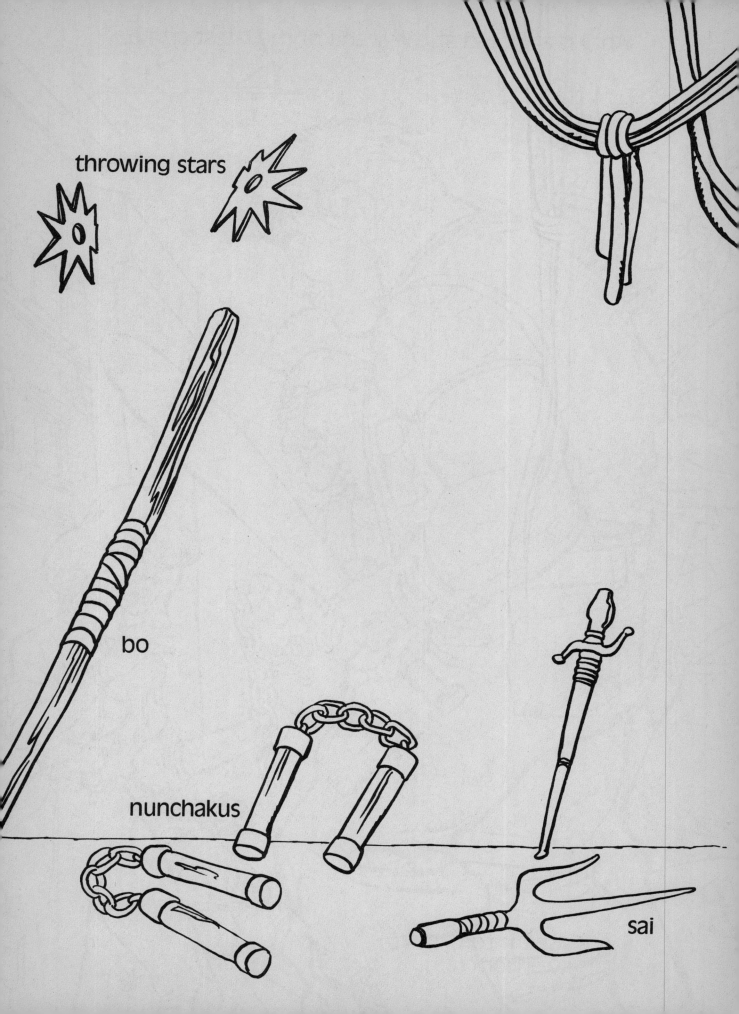

throwing stars

bo

nunchakus

sai

April is attacked at the scene of the latest crime.

"The Shredder asked us to tell you to mind your own business!" screams one punk.

April can escape to only one place.

But the punks follow her! The Teenage Mutant Ninja Turtles come to April's rescue just as she reaches a dead end in the sewer tunnel.

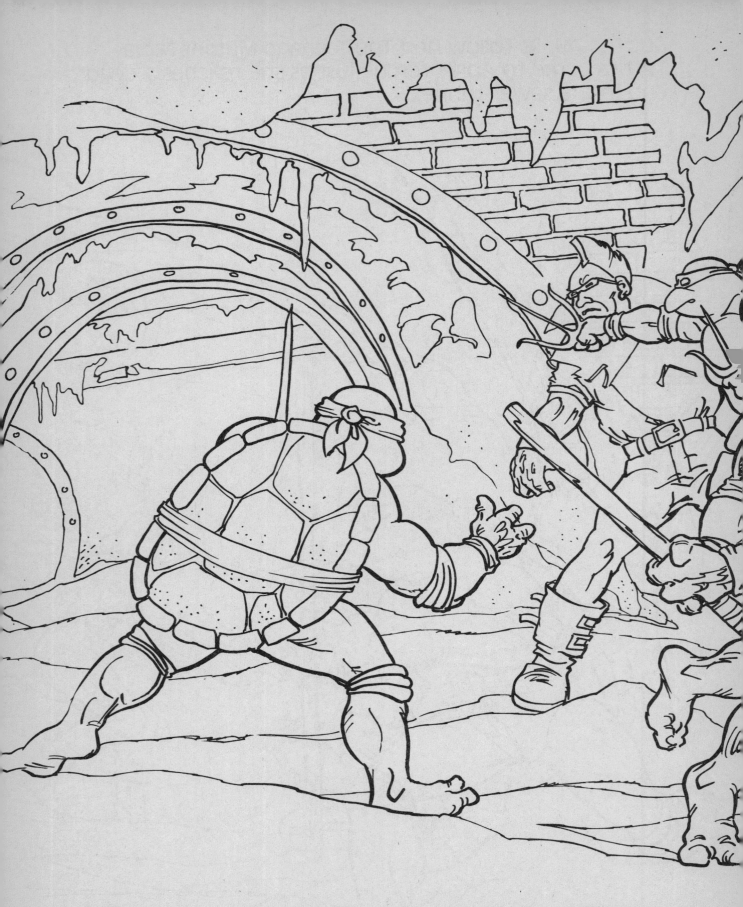

The turtles are very strong and are trained in the Ninja fighting arts. They live in the sewers with their Ninja master, Splinter.

"That was quick work. I could go for a pizza," says
Michaelangelo. Raphael sees a clue and picks it up.

April faints when she sees who her rescuers are.

The turtles bring April home to Splinter. Splinter was once a _shidoshi_, a great Ninja teacher, named Hamato Yoshi.

When April awakens, Splinter tells her about when he was a human named Yoshi, and how an enemy forced him to leave Japan.

"When the honored master <u>sensei</u> came to visit, I was unable to bow because of the dagger pinning my robe to the wall. But an even greater disgrace was to come," says Splinter.

"I pulled out the dagger to free myself. And I was accused of plotting against the <u>sensei's</u> life!" explains Splinter.

Yoshi came to America. Poor and friendless, he lived in the sewers with only rats to keep him company.

One day someone dumped four baby turtles into the sewer.

Yoshi and the turtles were very happy together until one terrible day. Something else came down the sewer—a chemical mutagen.

The mutagen made Yoshi more like the rats that surrounded him. But the turtles became more humanoid and grew very quickly.

Yoshi trained the turtles in the art of <u>ninjitsu</u>. As Ninja warriors they could protect themselves from outsiders who would call them freaks.

Yoshi named the turtles after his favorite Renaissance painters:

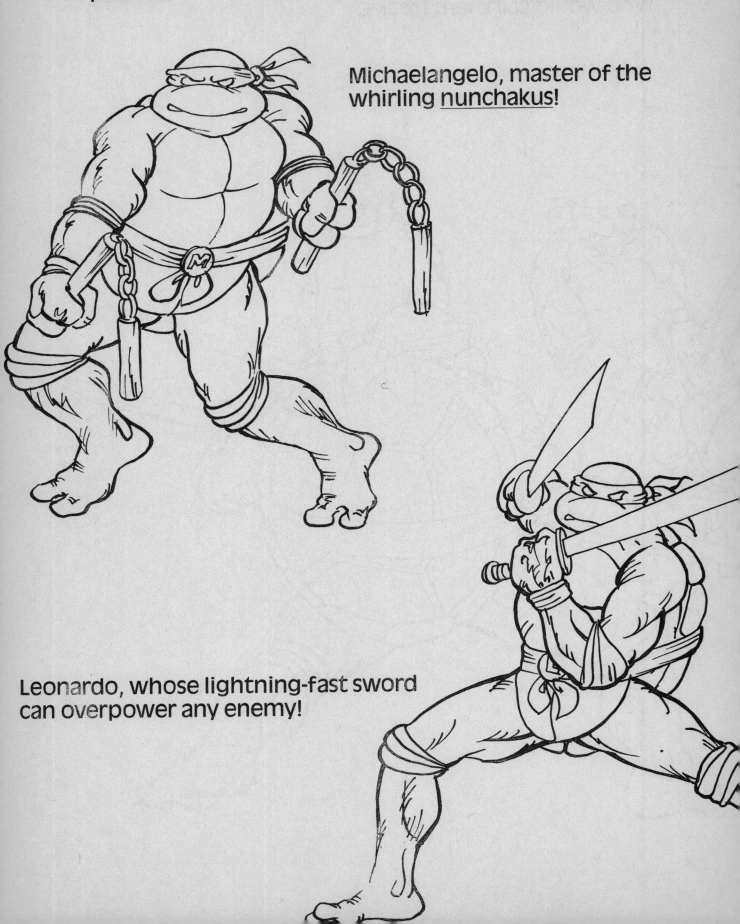

Michaelangelo, master of the whirling <u>nunchakus!</u>

Leonardo, whose lightning-fast sword can overpower any enemy!

Raphael, whose <u>sai</u> can overcome any weapon!

And Donatello, whose simple wooden <u>bo</u> is all-powerful in his hands!

The turtles gave Yoshi the new name Splinter. His hands and sharp new teeth could splinter blocks of wood.

"I believe the chemical that changed us was the work of my old enemy, who now calls himself the Shredder and disguises himself with an evil metal mask. He followed me to this country and now brings shame upon all Ninjas with his criminal activities," says Splinter.

"The Shredder! That's who sent those punks to threaten me! He's behind all the robberies!" says April.

"I think I know where we can find the Shredder. One of the punks dropped this card with the address of the Ninja Pizzeria on it," says Raphael.

The turtles and April set out to find the Ninja Pizzeria— and the Shredder!

But first the turtles must disguise themselves.

At the Ninja Pizzeria, the turtles order four pizzas with the works.

The Shredder is watching them through a hidden camera. He recognizes April.

"I want that newswoman brought back here. Now!" the Shredder screams to his Ninja robots.

While the turtles eat their pizzas, April goes outside to make a phone call.

The Shredder's Ninja robots, called footbots, kidnap April.

"Where's April?" the turtles wonder.

The turtles follow the trail.

"Heads up!" cries Raphael.

The good news is that April is still on the roof. The bad news is that she's surrounded by the Shredder's nasty footbots.

"Hey! These aren't Ninjas, they're robots!" calls Raphael.

Some footbots escape. The turtles and April follow
them in the hopes of finding the Shredder.

Far down a hallway, the turtles and April see the
Shredder. But before they can reach him, he throws a
switch and floods the hallway with water.

Suddenly part of the building starts to move! The
Shredder's headquarters is really a giant tank.

The turtles and April return to Splinter and tell him, "The Shredder is all washed up."

"The Shredder is sly and tricky," warns Splinter. "I have a feeling that we haven't seen the last of him...yet."